AF449099

LIVING ON
poems on grief and loss

LIVING ON
poems on grief and loss

Curated by
SWATI PAL

Hawakal
PUBLISHERS
New Delhi | Calcutta

Hawakal Publishers

70 B/9 Amritpuri, East of Kailash, New Delhi 65
33/1/2 K B Sarani, Mall Road, Calcutta 80

Email info@hawakal.com
Website www.hawakal.com

Cover designed by Bitan Chakraborty

First edition (paperback) August 2022

Copyright Living On © Hawakal 2022
Copyright Poems © Individual Contributors 2022

All rights reserved. No part of this publication may be reproduced or transmitted (other than for purposes of review/ critique) in any form or by any means, electronic or mechanical, including photocopy, recording, or any information storage and retrieval system without prior permission in writing from the publisher, editor, or the copyright holders where applicable.

ISBN: 978-93-91431-57-0 (paperback)

Price: INR 350 | USD 15.99

for
Ananya, Surya, Akul,
Divya, Tejaswee, Manorama (Maharaj),
Ananth, Rishikesh and Reba,
Mahadeb *&* Divakar (Mohan) —
you live on in us and we live on with you in our hearts

INTRODUCTION

If there is one thing that we have not learnt or been taught, it is to deal with grief. The grief that accompanies the loss of those we love. We do not know how to combat it or cope with it; indeed, we do not know how to accept it. If we are not ourselves struck by grief, we do not know how to handle someone who actually is suffering. We do not know what to say, how to act. Sometimes we offer advice or sermons or philosophy, especially relating to karma. And finally, we get on with our lives. Eventually, the one in grief finds herself / himself quite alone at the best of times as one by one, people start evading or avoiding or fobbing her/him off. Once the immediacy of the loss wears out, the person in grief is left with the feeling that people appear to have forgotten the loss and moved on with their lives. Aloneness swamps the person in grief. That loneliness adds to the terrible whiplash of grief. The feeling that one has been singled out in some way, simply grows and often a grief struck person becomes a recluse, is severely depressed and when it becomes unbearable, is suicidal.

I know this only too well.

A group of mothers who have lost their child/children are now my soul sisters; in them, I see a mirror image of myself and all I feel. And so also with others I know who are enduring loss and subsequent agony — every teardrop from their eyes makes me shed tears too. I want to wrap my arms around all of my soul sisters. I want to erase their pain. And yes, mine too. But is that even possible? Perhaps not. The greater the love, the more intense the pain, the pain of loss. But I could not sit by and see the misery. I could not let the anguish annihilate the souls of those whose affliction I understood keenly. They held my hand and I theirs. And I realized that all of us wanted the same thing — that those who we love and have lost physically, live on. That we immortalize them and how else to do that but through penning our pain, through inking our tears?

This was the birth of *Living On*. These are all poems of grief. They are all attempts to make those we love and who live in our hearts, live on in the memories of all, forever. In another sense, the poems are also about us; we who have lost our sense of self with the person(s) we have lost. We have to live on. Only if we do, and in the best that we can be of ourselves, will our loved ones be remembered.

SWATI PAL
July 2022
New Delhi

CONTENTS

Ananya Das

BHRAMAR CHOUDHURY

Bhramar lost her elder daughter, Ananya, about whom she writes:

Just like a freshly bloomed rose, soaked in the dewdrops of dawn—

She is my Tinni (Ananya). Just like the serene breeze of spring is her presence. She is brighter than a thousand suns. She is as patient as Mother Earth, as powerful and confident as a mountain rock. She walks like a plumed peacock on a monsoon day. My Tinni is an unending sea of love. She knows no hatred, enmity, or cruelty. She is a mother incarnate, an ideal daughter, wife, sister, teacher, and a person who embodies all things good and bright. I see her everywhere. All that is good in the world reminds me of her.

She was my eldest. She gave me the greatest gift of all — she made me a mother. She was my closest friend, a rock by my side. I was only 20 when she came into my life. Always gentle, always kind, always holding my hand — she taught me to love unconditionally and gave me more love than I ever knew existed. Not a single harsh word ever came out of her lips. Her laughter filled my home with joy. As years wore on, she cared for me like a mother. She was my *Sakhi*, my confidante, my soul-mate. For me, my Tinni lives on. She has gone nowhere. She is waiting for me somewhere, I know. And every night, before I fall asleep, I hear her say — *"Ma, ami acchi. Tumi ghumao"* (*Ma, I am here, you sleep*).

Ananya Das was an accomplished motivational speaker and life-coach. She had over 30 years of management experience in information technology. She worked in senior managerial positions at many multinational corporations, such as Birla Soft, Sapient, and Snap O Business Solutions. She excelled in the fields of IT, and HR and in her last years, worked as Chief Information Security Officer at a reputed IT firm in Gurgaon. Ananya was also a guest faculty in management at the Institute of Social Welfare and Business Management (IISWBM), Calcutta University, and a few reputed engineering colleges. She had her own training and consultancy firm, *Sopaan,* which she set up on social entrepreneurship. She was a gold medalist in her postgraduate and MPhil batches at Calcutta University.

She passed away of a heart ailment in the process of publishing her book, *Rise To The Top*. However, her legacy lives on in the form of her many short stories, blogs on leadership and motivation, and her book.

LAST WORDS

They say
No word ever is lost.
Words are immortal, indestructible
Words are
"Shabda Brahma" (Sound God)

Her last words were :
"Maa, I am okay, Maa."

Those words must be alive too
Somewhere,
Somewhere.
Are they?

I listen carefully,

Silently
Helplessly.

I want to hear her words.
But they have left my ears
Escaped this mundane earth
Lost in some unknown, unreachable

Ether.

PAIN

Give me pain
So much pain
That the earth
Can hold me no more

Then
Enclose the last flicker
Of my candle.
See how it melts itself,
To write
its tale of pain
on the pages of darkness.
Like I.

Give me pain

To write.

THIS PAIN

This sharp, penetrating pain,
Is like the shaft of hail that
tears the sail of my boat.

Let there be thunder and rain,
Then see,
How the sapling of hope
Irrigated by
The blood of my aching heart,
Sprouts life.

The axis of the earth
The unceasing
Balance of light and dark

Moves around
The orbit of my pain.

And becomes
Universal.

O SKY !

O sky
Why are you crying so incessantly?
Has your dear daughter
Left you too ?

That curly hair
That innocent lovely face,
Honey sprinkled smile
Carelessly dressed,
Bright intelligent eyes
Suffused with love.

Was your daughter
Like mine?
Has she left you too?
Is that why you
burst with so much tears?

Is that why
You flood the earth?

Is that why your
 heart wails in thunder
 burns in lightning?

But O firmament!
You are not as luckless
As I

You have hope

This grass drenched in rain

These crotons, palms, krishnachuras
Are green and red and yellow with your tears

These pink petals of Madhabi
Are fragrant with your tears.

The earth returns to you
As clouds
And makes you blue
Again.
The sun is also you.
And me?

I am
A vacuum
My tears do not
Bring her alive.
My curly-haired, fairy-like
Darling daughter

Will never return
Again.

MY MEMORIES

Memories, my memories
are an endless shower of rain
falling incessantly
On my desert-heart.
And make my arid bosom moist.
In your embalming, embracing arms
let me sob silently.

Memories, my memories
Of my baby
Come to me like a gush of strong wind
Come and sway me away
Like lifeless fallen dry leaves
To nowhere.

Memories, my memories
Like a bunch of Rajanigandha
Fill me with the fragrance of the past.
Let me close my eyes
And feel your loving presence
Around me, my loving Tinni.

Memories ,my memories
I have kept you with care
In every drop of my blood.

Promise me, my darling girl
That you will flow out of my pen
And be a poem or a story
About a mother and a daughter
Or their union and separation

Of how life
Makes
And

Falls.

SHE

She
Went away stealthily.
As spring leaves the earth
As colours leave the trees
In summer

She left.

How can she,
Always so present
Be merged
With nothingness?

Then.
She comes back,
Flooding my eyes
Flashing a torchlight in one hand
And holds mine with the other.
She readies me for a journey
From unreal to real
From darkness to light
From death to immortality.

She was, she is, and ever she will
Remain my North Star.

Surya Panda

ANITA PANDA

Anita lost her brother, Late Col Surya Panda. She writes about him:

As a little boy, he loved to play with the Army toy tank gifted to him by our globe-trotter father. That probably sowed early within him the seeds of a fierce passion to join the armed forces and serve his motherland. He was a die-hard patriot, a profound and mature thinker, an award-winning poet, an ace athlete, adventurist, cricketer and a gifted actor and director of plays at his alma-mater. Surya, my brother, comrade-in-childhood crime, mentor, counsellor, critic and confidante was no ordinary soul! He was a man of exceptional courage and wisdom. A valiant officer and a gentleman. As gentle as he was strong! He touched so many lives in so many ways in his short and eventful life.

From the icy Kargil heights to the bloody woods of J & K, the humid jungles of the North-East to the scorching deserts of Thar, he fought each counter-insurgency operation on India's borders as boldly as the ominous, lethal enemy within, devouring his cells greedily. He was a Warrior! He battled cancer with a stoic smile, supreme positivity and heroic valour, meeting his demons head-on and viewed even his critical illness as "a great learning in pain management", as he would say. Honed by years of gruelling military training and innate courage.

His words — "Keep the soldier in you alive and intact always" on World Cancer Day defined his robust attitude!

He aced his exam and earned his MBA degree from IIM Lucknow even post his critical six-hour surgery for 'Malignant Melanoma' on November 13, 2018. Amongst his many achievements, in a dare-devil feat, Surya was instrumental in safely bringing down a 'sick' Army chopper from a high-altitude glacier down to the base camp in 'Op Vijay', Kargil in 1999-2001. He was a real life Hero!

An optimist and fighter to the core, Surya succumbed to cancer in the early hours of 9th January, 2021 at Fortis Hospital, Noida. He went down but not without one last fierce fight! This brave son of the nation was draped in the tri-colours of our national flag and cremated with full military honours. He departed in true military style befitting a true soldier.

The heavens are richer with Surya, the brilliant, radiant sun and that brightest star twinkling brightest like a guardian angel. He fought well and invincibly. For, soldiers never die! RIP Beloved Brother.

MOURNING YOU

When you mourn a flower deeply,
You mourn away its withering away too.
With every petal falling away
Drifting silently down
A piece of your heart dies too…

Today you have come home,
Adorned in a gilded photo frame
Gazing at me intensely with your gentle half-smile
Speaking silently, wordlessly.
Penetrating deep into my soul…

My sibling, my mentor and counselor.
My childhood partner-in-crime!
Those playful squabbles and banters
Endless tiffs and arguments.
Yet covering up and standing up for me!

My defender and protector always!
I feel and sense your presence all around
Walking behind, beside, and ahead of me.
Leading the way always
Formless, invisible but forever there.

You are NO MORE!

Living On

No more in body
But engraved in me eternally.

Perhaps with angels now!
Or, in some faraway land?
Busy playing your new afterlife role.
Do you yearn too?
For me and all your loved ones as we do?

The grief flows in torrential rivulets,
Like the furious, pelting rain.
Mingling with the salt of my tears
Sabotaging my peace and joy
Of your homecoming as a framed avatar.

I miss YOU Brother!
I long for your presence and guidance.
Your chiding and admonishing
Your words of wisdom and prudence
Do you miss me too???

For now it is enough,
To have you here with me in this gilded photo frame
Until we reunite again
And rejoice in sibling revelry
Forever and eternally in your secure realm…

LIFE YOU CAN BREAK ME

Life you can break me!
Through every trial and torture you throw at me
Baring your lethal fangs
With sinister glee!

The wounds are raw and bleeding,
Maybe not yet healed!
The heart and soul are maimed and wounded
Under your trampling feet
But I will not be a victim or cry!
Fight and arise I will again and again each time you break me!

My heart was born an invincible warrior!
Each day I will fight on still.
Each horrifying darkness, grief and pain
Each challenge, tragedy, sorrow and loss
I will face with undaunted will!

Life you can choke, churn and whiplash me!
With your cruel might and power
But I will fight each time with all my will!
Withstand every storm that blinds me
I will arise, prevail and triumph still!

TONIGHT

Tonight is the night,
The longest and most agonising one
As my sibling battles in the ICU
Oblivious to his loved ones
Fervently praying for his precious life.

So many battles he fought valiantly,
From the icy Kargil heights,
The beautiful, bloody woods of the Nort-East
To the scorching deserts of Thar!
But tonight he fights a lethal war, an insidious foe.

Worse than those he fought on the nation's borders
From within his own body
Devouring and mutating his cells greedily…

My childhood pal and playmate
My comrade-in-crime, mentor, brother and confidante.
A wealth of memories, secrets and shared dreams
A bond unbreakable
And beyond lifetimes…

Tonight will be a long and dark night!
Dark like the inky sky,
Dotted with countless stars, galaxies and planets

That shift and revolve
And decide the twists and turns of human fate!

Tonight is the night

As his kith-and-kin wait with bated breath
A night of tests and trials by fire!
A test of our patience and faith.
As my brother valiantly and silently battles
The grim and sinister foe within…

Tonight is the deadly, horrific night!
As we wait, pray, chant and hope
For him to bounce back.
For a miracle, surreal.

So many more battles more
He must fight and win!
So many more laughs and tears still to be shared
So many more paths to traverse together
Fight on my Brother Surya!

For soldiers never die…

SOLDIERS NEVER DIE

The Brave one fought and how!
Undaunted until his last breath.
Fighting the lethal, ominous enemy lurking within
Masking the crushing pain, fatigue, nausea and blue,
chipped nails
With a brave heart's smile!

He fought and how each battle with supreme positivity!
From the icy Kargil heights to the Siachen Glacier
From the beautiful, bloody woods of Kashmir to the
scorching deserts of Thar
He fought each battle on the LOCs

And within his frail body
Fighting the invisible enemy within
Devouring his cells and organs greedily
Spreading like a ravaging fire.

He fought and how!
Each attack of the insidious foe
Baring its fangs in glee.
Calm and strong, unfazed and indefatigable!

Braving the painful rounds of treatment with a stoic smile
Bearing each needle piercing his frail body

An optimist and Warrior to the core.
He fought and how!

Until his last breath on the ventilator in the cold ICU!
Supine, limbs swollen, lesioned liver, lungs and spleen.
Breathless and with eyes glazed
But not without one last fierce fight!

And then he departed in true military style!
Draped in the tri-colours of the national flag
Cremated with full military honours
And a glorious gun salute!

An officer, gentleman and true soldier
Immortal and forever eternal…
He lives on in the stars, earth, oceans, wind and fire now.
He lives on in every memory, song, smile of yesteryears.
In the hearts he touched with compassion.

He lives on through his legacy of courage and valour
As gentle as he was strong!
Gone from this earthly realm now,
Merging into the infinite cosmos
So, becoming clouds he can return again and again to
Mother earth.

He lives on through his indomitable spirit,
RIP Beautiful and brave soul!
For soldiers never die!

FAREWELL BRAVEHEARTS

Thirteen coffins lay at Palam,
Thirteen families grieved in silence
Draped in their country's tri-colours.
Pristine wreaths placed upon them
With petals strewn and showered.

They, the great and valiant men in uniform
The Warriors and Heroes who fought guarding our borders
With their invincible valour
Gone and lost in swift seconds
In a cruel twist of fate!

The air is solemn and sombre,
A billion hearts crushed and aggrieved
The nation mourns in deep anguish
As the flames leap high with the pyres lit
The collective grief rising like the leaping fire
But neither fire, wind nor water can erase their valour!

Farewell Bravehearts!
We mourn and feel your shocking and colossal loss
The last rites are done.
Your bodies now handfuls of ashes
Merging into the great cosmos…

But one day again,
You great souls will come back to this earth
To don the uniforms and earn those glorious medals again!
Your lives, journeys and courage folklore
Rest in peace for now.
Farewell Bravehearts…

THE SCARS I WEAR

The wounds I bear bleeding in my heart,
The scars I wear as my badges of honour
The crushing sorrow, loss of love and betrayal,
The trials by fire, the pain and trauma
The battles I have fought, the tears of despair
Branded on my soul are the scars I wear
My scars of honour!

The lethal disease the brave one fought,
The shattering divorce, the loss of a loved one no more!
The shock and denial, the tidal rage and helplessness
The suffering and mourning that left us scarred
Are the badges of honour I proudly wear!

The grief that softened me.
The heart-break that wisened me.
The suffering that strengthened me.
Ah! All the scars that I now wear
Are branded on my heart like medals!!!

KS Thimayya

JAYA AIYAPPA

Jaya lost her elder son, Akul, and this is what she writes about him:

Akul aka Captain KS Thimayya was a pilot, but in his own words, "I am not just a pilot." A trekker, slack liner, paraglider, cyclist he donned many hats.

Akul was born on 26 March 1989, early morning on Easter Sunday. This Easter Bunny bright eyed and smiling brought all the love and happiness and changed our lives. When he was a kid, many people said, "They don't make them like him anymore". Gentle, sensitive, caring, he always put others before him. Akul had to be taught to hit back. He never harmed anyone. There are numerous instances when he has undergone hardships to put others at ease even as a little child. I remember a mother narrating how he gave his raincoat to her daughter so that she would not get wet in the rain and he walked home alongside her covering himself with his school bag. He was only 7 years old then.

Akul's childlike enthusiasm for even the smallest of things was rare. Simple pleasures like a perfectly ripe avocado, guava, pineapple or any other fruit would make him so excited and jump with joy. His search for the perfectly brewed aromatic cup of coffee was an ongoing project. A simple home cooked meal was his favourite. He loved his food but enjoyed having family and friends along with him to share it. Generous to a fault, his house had an open invitation for all at any time. His larder was full and the bar well stocked, even though he was a teetotaller. Since he didn't drink he was always the person who made sure everyone reached home safe after an enjoyable outing.

Akul's knowledge on subjects was at times baffling. One could talk with him about — laddu's for lactating women or electronics, especially anything to do with a Mac, or his favourite sport Formula 1 racing, or about watches, machinery and almost anything. His research on topics was thorough and made him the go to person for all friends and family. All vacations and trips were planned by him to the minutest detail. Unfortunately, he did not plan his last trek.

As a professional, Akul got his pilot's license before his driver's license. When he was a co-pilot, sitting on the right seat, other captains could depend on him, as he would have completed all the checks properly and thoroughly. He took his responsibilities seriously. A pilot and a gentleman, who always had everyone's best wishes on his mind, everyone including drivers, cabin crew, ground staff, all came to pay their respects and say a final goodbye to him. The standard set by him was so high that many times, he was used as a benchmark by others while training the novices.

Akul, the friend — reliable, encouraging, always present, always there when someone needed him. There are many instances of how he has been there for people suffering from depression called them and encouraged them to get back to the jobs, some even pilots. He has helped others deal with their anxieties of flying and talked people into doing things which they would be scared to. He believed in making other people's special days more special by making sure he attended weddings, birthdays, celebrations and he always took part in all the festivities and helped organise them. How he made time for everyone and made everyone feel important, remains a mystery.

Akul's favourite festival was undoubtedly Holi. It involved planning so that he could be at his favourite place with all his friends and enjoy it the way he did as a child. That was Akul, who would take the effort to have fun and include as many friends as he could. His love for outdoors as well as indoors is known. He could spend a day cycling or slack lining and end it with a game of Catan, as long there were others with him.

Akul, a free spirit seemed like he wanted to do so much and be in so many places. He lived his life by loving, laughing and leaving behind warm happy memories for all his family and friends.

Akul, there really isn't another like you.

TRIUMPH OF EVIL

It's Dusherra
The day good triumphed over evil
But what's good
Who decides

It can't be
A kid gone before time
Not yet enjoyed life fully
And me still here.

It's evil
To leave me here
And take him away.

It seems
Evil triumphed.

CONNECTION

2G, 3G, 4G even 5G
Which connection is best

Mobile, I pad, laptop
Internet or calls
Zoom, meet, or skype
Which is the best way to connect.

The best connection
The only life time connection
The unbreakable connection
Is only

The umbilical cord

JOY VS SADNESS

The contractions came
Quicker and quicker
The pain
The unbearable pain
But soon
I had a bundle of joy
A baby boy
N I knew it before anyone else in the world

What joy
What perfection that baby was
Holding him in my arms
Looking into his face
I was content
Excited, happier than ever before

I held him in my arms again
For the last time ever
The beautiful baby
Now a handsome young man
Looking into his face
I was lost
Desolate, numb, sadder than ever before.

DEAL WITH IT

Meditate they say
It calms the mind
Work for the under privileged
Give your life a purpose.

Heal your self
Make a difference
Find the reason to go on.

Grief
Trauma
Deal with it
Religion, Humanity, Chants, Spirituality
What does one do

Cleanse myself of trauma
Of grief
They say
But
How do I
Cleanse myself of love.

PROUD MAMA

'Make me proud', he said
And I did win a prize.
For you, my dear
I said, smilingly.

Are you proud today
Of me
Eating, drinking, working.
Crying, howling, breaking down
And still carrying on.

But,
No one is prouder than me
For having carried you
For giving you birth
For holding you
For calling you my son

For knowing
That
You will be my baby forever.

45

CAPTAIN

'Cabin crew to be seated for landing'
The captains voice comes over the speakers.
The touch down,
Smooth and on time,
Everyone's smiling.

Then why
Why
Are there tears rolling down my cheeks
Unstoppable tears,
Others wondering what's wrong.

I remember
When it was your voice over the speakers
So confident, so in control
And I was assured
Nothing could ever go wrong.

What do I tell the others
It was you here the last time
The captain was you.

Divya Prasad Ambashta

JAYA PRASAD

Jaya lost her elder sister, Divya. And she writes about her thus:

I hadn't imagined even in my wildest dream that one day I would sit down to write her obituary. Now as I do so, I don't know how I can summarise her in just ten lines or a page. She deserved life and happiness but it was not to be. Her life was defined by struggle at the hands of people who had unmitigated dislike and hatred for her because she was born to fortune. The fact that she had affluent parents made her a victim of jealousy of those who lived off her parent's money. The saga was not limited to her parental family but continued in her marital home too. She died of negligence emanating from marital discord. Even her well meant efforts were misunderstood. All her efforts within the four walls of her home were rudely rebuffed and rejected. She died an agonized soul, frustrated and disappointed.

She was Divya Prasad Ambashta.

For me she was just Didi. Born as the second child of our parents,Radha Mohan Prasad and Kusum Verma, Didi was blessed with an indomitable spirit that irked her detractors no end. Yes she died but not without giving a fight. Her life was full of day-to-day struggle yet she never allowed the pains inflicted on her to harden her heart. She was a tender and pious woman. God had thrown umpteen troubles in her path but she remained devout till her last breath. She was a worshipper of Goddess Durga and Shiv. It was noticed on that dark evening in May when her ashes were being immersed that the holy Ganga had miraculously risen by a feet or two as if eager to quickly receive her daughter and free her from the pains of the human world.

Didi never allowed her sensitivity to die even as she faced the insensitivity and cruelty of people. Didi was a philanthropist, feeding street urchins and needy villagers. She was gifted with vision and foresight and one could depend on her for the right advice and also for help in times of need.

She was a modern educated woman and a budding entrepreneur. She was gifted with amazing aesthetic sense and creativity and it was her dream to run her own boutique. Her passion became her nemesis and gave her detractors, both her disgruntled kith and kin and outsiders, to pin her down and ultimately push her towards death. Didi was a well meaning and sincere woman intentionally not understood and victimized by the manipulators in her life. She was courageous, raising her voice against all that was wrong in her own life and outside. Her death has badly shaken our belief and faith in the Almighty. She deserved to live surrounded by people who loved and valued her unconditionally. She has left a void that can never be filled.

SUDDENLY

Suddenly
The eyes water
Suddenly a smile stops
Suddenly
The heart skips a beat
Suddenly
The picture floats
Across the mind
Suddenly
As Durga
As Sati
As Savitri
Suddenly
You flow
As tears from my eyes
Didi...

FRAMED

Your pulsating persona
Stands framed
In a corner
Magenta silk saree
With golden border
A puja thali
Full of flowers and incense
A young bride
Frail and beautiful
Wide eyed
Stands relegated
Framed and frozen
With all the stillness
The cacophony of existence
Silenced
What is left behind?
A frozen heart
Loaded with frozen tears
Sinking and sinking
In the ocean of your memory
While the world stands at the shore
Fresh and free
A new lease of life
In your death
Your pulsating persona
Stands framed
In a corner darling…

YOU AND ME

You will live
As long as I live
You can't go
For I am here
I carry you
In me
In my heart
In my mind
In my soul
You will come
To hold my hand again
Some day
In some way
You can't leave
You can't go
I won't allow you
To just vanish in thin air
You can't do what you did
You have to come back
To finish the journey
On a happy note
My lovely sis
I have many stories to tell
Many secrets to share
I have lots of complain to make
And patch ups too
And where are my gifts ?

Living On

That I demanded from you?
Those promises and plans ?
My lovely sis ?
You will live
As long as I live
My lovely sis...
You are here
For I am here.
You will never become
A forgotten story
A song not heard fully
You will live
For I live
My lovely sis...

THE LAST EMBRACE

Up in flames
In wind and water
You went,
I left you with the last embrace
My heart touching yours,
Your softness has lingered
In my arms.

I search for you frantically
Desperate I rush out
In wind and water
Hoping to feel you
Through wind and water
The breeze
The rain
All seem to sing your song
Didi ....

The birds and flowers
All carry your colours ..
Didi...

That one last time
Will linger long
When the roles got horribly reversed...
You were in the arms
Of your first kiddo

Living On

Your youngest sibling,
Fearless and carefree I grew
Pampered in sisterly shade
Made of love and care
Your wide and beautiful eyes
I cannot forget
The care and comfort
That I felt in them...
The warmth has lingered
Of the last embrace
Of my love lying in my arms....
Didi

WRAPPED IN LOVE

The clouds were dark
The rains came down
Beating at my heart
The threatening lightening
Ready to strike
My eyes flooded
My face quivered
Then you floated in my dream
Gracious and calm
Placidity around
Serenity
Gently softly
You sailed
Leaving me behind
I rose at dawn
Wrapped in love
Didi....

DECEIVING GODS

Could you tell me
God !
What went wrong?
The multiple 'why'(s) & 'how'(s)
Crowd my mind
Mist my eyes
As I stand before you
God!
Dumbfounded
Stunned
Numbed
Mechanical
Confused
Dazed
Fumbling for words
I sing your praise
Mutter prayers
Nothing nothing
Soothes my aching heart
God !
Could you tell me
What went wrong?
She fumbled
Or you fumbled
Or we humble beings
Were at fault ?
Could you tell me

God !
What went wrong?
She sang praises less
Or YOU the Almighty
Were too busy to hear her calls ?
Didi....

Tejaswee Rao

SEEMA TEJASWEE RAO

Seema lost her daughter, Tejaswee, and writes about her:

Beginning in the summer of 1990, we monitored 'the baby's' growth, reading 'Pregnancy' by Gordon Bourne, (no internet then) jotting down the dates eagerly as the baby grew inside, imagining who she would look like, as the book told us that baby's eye lashes and nails had started to appear, unseen but already adored. We were enthusiastic first- time parents. Reading — because the baby must love books; trying meditation, going for walks, dancing, and listening to Tanpura, because the baby was listening and learning.

When she was born on 19.1.91 (a palindrome), the first thing I noticed about her was her deep, delightful dimples. Tejaswee was an extrovert. Even as a toddler she chattered nonstop. She was already speaking in short sentences at 14 months ("Wanna go down", "Draw Mickey", "Read-to-Tejhee")... A mother I met in a toddler's park said, "Speaking too early brings bad luck." I wasn't even remotely superstitious or concerned. She was safe from all bad luck because what could be more powerful than a mother's love!

Tejaswee loved being read to as a toddler, amongst her many favorites was James Herriot, not surprisingly; she wanted to be a vet when she grew up. At one and a half, when I was visiting my parents, my dad took her for a walk and she returned with three delighted, excited puppies (from the street corner) in her tiny, chubby arms!

At ten, she spotted from her school bus, two kittens, one on a branch hanging inside a drain, another on the edge. They were still there hours later when the school bus was dropping them back home. The teachers and the driver didn't agree to let her get down and help them. She reached home looking so distraught that we drove back, sure she misunderstood what she saw, not even sure she would remember exactly where she saw them. But the kittens were found and brought home, washed, fed and adopted. On her behalf, I was angry with all the others who saw but did nothing.

I felt helpless too. How was she going to survive in this world? This world didn't deserve such sensitive children. But Tejaswee did not feel helpless. I was grateful for that! Pest control at home was always humane, involving no killing, because we were the ones invading their habitat. She continued to bring home many kittens and puppies, one baby squirrel, one owl (rescued from crows). In her first year in college, she volunteered at an animal shelter, and it was heart breaking to see how disturbed she sometimes was, when she couldn't really help an animal in pain. She was capable, willing to go all out, and compassionate, and the compassion included whoever needed it.

How was she going to survive in this world full of terrible cruelty? How could I imagine!? She was already as much a friend as a daughter, she was a confidante and advisor too. My cup was full. I felt blessed, grateful and content.

Tejaswee was never without a book. I read on her recommendation, *Chocolat* by Joanne Harris, and P Sainath's *Everybody Loves a Good Drought*. And, *Shantaram...* which I read two years after I could ever tell her I didn't like. That would have been a discussion.

Tejaswee read and she wrote. At 14, she had started writing a sequel to one of the Harry Potter books and I found a letter to J K Rowling assuring her that she was "just 14, and no threat to your writing career." Some reassurance for J K Rowling.

At 15, in a school assignment, she wrote "A Letter to the Future," which she later shared on her blog. She meant what she had written. This letter sums up Tejaswee.

Dear… daughter,

I don't feel odd writing this. Just… so mature. I'm 17 going on 18, the age you'll be when you read this for the first time. I don't know how I'll be then. Sometimes cranky, over-worked, cynical, the way I see my parents are today. But I don't want you to see only that me. Maybe I'll be hardworking, happy and eccentric. For you, I want to preserve some of my ideas, my optimism and my ideals. I want you to meet me, at your age, so many years from now. Beware… I was considered boring by some.

Right now I'm changing. In small ways, and big. I've seen a certain amount of heartbreak (no doubt I'll see more) and a great deal of love, more than I could ever wish for. My morals, my ideals, my resolutions, my wants and my beliefs are being formed, being broken, and formed again with a stronger base. I want to be the President of India. I want to take 6 months off before college. I want to be the most powerful person on earth. I want to spend the rest of my life helping the poor. I want to adopt a girl and I know this is one resolution that won't be broken. So you're the one… It's wonderful to meet you.

I wonder… are you flummoxed by Physics as I am? Do you paint like I do? Who is your role model? Do you know the history of your family? Or your country? Are you loud, like me, or quiet, like your grandmother? I can hear her soft laugh in the next room. Will she still be laughing like that many years from now? There are so many things I want to tell you, things I don't want to forget, and fear I will. Things that may be 'too trivial' in another five years…

Look at yourself carefully every morning. Red streaks, or two plaits; Fat or skinny; knobby knees, or gorgeous legs; Small eyes or mosquito-bite breasts; I want you to be proud of yourself, exactly the way you are. And I want you to remember that, what's inside, is a thousand times more valuable than what's outside. I've learnt that from my mother, but will she be there to teach you the same? The world will love you and hate you for what you do and what you think. So make sure your thoughts and your actions are stable and reliable and valued enough (by you) to keep you steady and give you strength through anything the world throws at you.

I want you to be bold as I am. Don't be afraid to stand up and fight when you feel that something's wrong, but know also when to hold back and keep silent. I've learnt this the hard way. I hope you don't have to.

Don't be scared of making mistakes. I am, but that doesn't stop me from making them all the time. It just makes me more conscious of every trip and stumble, when I pick myself up again.

Don't smoke. This is the one absolute I give you today. Don't start, because if you do, it will be difficult to quit, and you don't have to go through that.

I want you to have principles, and stick to them. If you believed something once, you had a reason to think that way. Don't let peer pressure make you forget what you once stood by. But don't be stubbornly resistant to change either.

Do you believe in God? I do.

I want you to know, that every day is a challenge, but that every time you walk out that door, there will be someone waiting for you to get home to whom you can proudly display your battle wounds. There will be people who'll try to change you to suit their needs, but for each of these, know that there are others who'll help you change to better yourself. Learn to recognise the difference. I took me ages... you won't always find people exactly like you, but no matter who you're with, be yourself.

I want you to read *To Kill a Mocking Bird* and watch *Life is Beautiful*.

You have to be strong and believe in yourself, like Atticus, but with that, never loose the innocence of Scout.

Never forget your ambitions, even the ones lost or changed. They have strange ways of cropping up again and fitting into your life. Am I a vet or an editor? Or do I work for the Indian Administrative Service?

Never, ever make the mistake of convincing yourself that your instinct is wrong. If something looks or feels wrong, then it most probably is. Trust your instinct. Remember the cat, Puppy? The one I told you about? If I haven't yet, then ask me… I once saved him with pure instinct. It's a long story.

Do I sound like a teenager to you?

Enjoy each day like it's the last one you'll live. Is this saying still a cliché?

One day you'll meet the guy you'll love. Maybe you've already met him. Wasn't it the headiest feeling in the world when he said he loved you? It was for me. But, also the scariest. It takes a trust I'm still learning to give.

I dream big, and I watch my dreams fall. Right now, I have the strength to rise.

Listen Kid, I love you. I've never seen you, but it's as if I'm talking to myself all over again.

Is this a selfish letter? In a way, yes, but it's heartfelt.

Lots of Love, xxx

At nineteen, in so many ways she was still a child, following me around, non stop chattering about her day, her dreams, her friends, her plans for the future.

I was the household paparazzi, following her around as she ate, read, dried her hair and even slept!

I used to wonder how some parents managed to be angry with their children, I could summon no anger at her. Maybe because there was so little time…

I just can't remember what name she had chosen for her

future daughter. She wanted to give her a short name that couldn't be further shortened. She had chosen Tj for herself, because she did not like Tejaswee being shortened to Teju.

This letter is precious to me. I imagine the "Letter to the Future" is Tejaswee's gift to us, that she is showing us how to cope. That is why we found such solace in our rainbow child, Kia Tejaswee, adopted two years after our world ended when we lost Tejaswee to dengue on Aug 11, 2010.

THE EARLIEST DAYS: BEYOND WORDS.

It's beyond anything imaginable
How do I explain?
This grief spills out of all dictionaries.
Not one word has the compassion
To hold its horror
Harrowing pales
Distress fails
Dread is devoid
Anguish is wanting
Sorrow doesn't come close to what it entails

Then how do I share?
They want to care
But no one seems to know
And I have no words to show
The endlessness of this pain
So much pain
That relationships cringe
Making me feel unhinged
Dazed
Terrified
Disoriented
Bewildered
The loneliness of not being understood!
Swamped.

Breathless.
Engulfed.
Drowning.
Sinking
Lost
And through it all,
Alone.
I can't breathe

And then I met another
Child gone and still a mother
Breathing in the same nightmare
And I needed no words to share

THE EARLIEST DAYS:THE HOPE

Nothing made sense.
She couldn't be 'no more'.
The two decades of meaning
All the purpose and the joy
The hugs and the endless chatter
The future!
How was I supposed to cope?
Could one breath without hope?
There had to be a way.
Think positive.
There is always a way.
Don't give up.
Connect somehow.
Let her know

The only way to cope
Was to find some hope

There was life after life
I know, I know
She lives forever in my heart
Couldn't I speak to her just once?
How was she?
Did she suffer?
I know she did…

Living On

One last hug.
A last goodbye
Please god,
Why create so much love to snatch it away?
There had to be a way
Find that way.
Do whatever it takes.
It's either this or…
Tell nobody.
Nobody gets it.
A trip to the Himalayas?
A child born on the same day?
Talk to her, aloud, she hears you.
A sign
A dream

Was this hope
Or beginning of insanity?
Was this still insanity
If this was the only way?
Millions have survived with make believe
Like prisoners of war!
Imagining food where there was none
Imagining joy
Amidst torture and death.
That was how it was done
I was drowning
Couldn't breathe with the endlessness of the end
But I could live with this make-believe.

She was here…
My little miracle
Flesh of my flesh
Grown inside me
Born out of me

Walked taller than me
Wiser than I could ever be
Loved and cherished
My raison de etre
She had to be somewhere
I would meet her again
Once, just once
Or else,
I could pretend.
I would pretend.

THE AUDACITY OF MY HOPE!

And I brush my teeth
And I smile
I think everyday thoughts
I breathe
And I bathe
I eat and I drink
She's not there
Never will be,
I think that and still manage to breath
Who can understand this?
That I wish I could just shut my eyes
And never open them again
That I wish I could see her just once
To say good bye
To tell her how much I loved her
And then I realize
She knew.
She knows.
She knows and she lets me know.
Precious words remembered,
Love outlives life
I exist because she does too
That's why I brush my teeth
And still manage to breathe

THE EARLIEST DAYS: IT'S LIKE…

Just close my eyes
Undo the past two weeks
And wake up two weeks ago.

It's like
Being packed inside a trunk
And the trunk kicked around,
And when I step out for a bit,
She's still not here.

It's like
Being stabbed and then being stabbed again
That weight in the center of my chest
A twisting knife cruelly pressed
I could live with the pain
If that weight was lifted

It's like
Drowning
Drowning
And when it became impossible
Unbearable
Still drowning
Then come up suddenly
Feel nothing

And then drowning again.

It's like
There's a jumbled yarn in my head
Telling me I have known gentle kicking beneath my ribs
I have known the wait
She had been 49 cms long
Born a day after the due date
She had grabbed my hair in her fist
I want her back
Let her be born to me again
My best friend
My confidante
She was my box full,
Room full,
Universe full of chocolate
When all I had dared ask for was one little candy

So
No way was this acceptable

Then the jumbled yarn in my head would wrap around
tighter
It had questions
Did I really ever have a child?
Yes?
Then where was she?
Was I alive?
Is this how being alive felt?
What was being alive?
Was this life worth the pain?
Was being a mother worth the pain?
Her pain
And now mine
Where was she

My Tejaswee
(Don't call out to her)
Was this world real?
Only two things were real
The pain and the confusion
Was everything an illusion?

And someone saying,
She's not crying
She must be in shock.

I TRY, I REALLY DO.

It's become a habit
To defend my sadness
Aloud,
Or in my mind.

The lessons don't seem to sink in.
The teachers know not what they teach.
Be positive
Act normal
Accept what can't be changed
Life doesn't stop for anybody
Serve the poor
Nobody likes a Pity Party
Count the blessings
Be grateful for what is left.
You have changed!

What does that mean?

I try to feel no pain
When a little head ambles past,
bent on a book, focused on reading

I try not to miss a step
When little girls on the kerb

kneel down to hug a stray pup

It's difficult not to miss
The ones I will never hold
When grandchildren laugh aloud
In parks
In books
On the TV
In conversations

It's an effort to keep breathing

When young cheeks
Burst into her dimples.
I have not yet learned not to be appalled
By a headful of her hair,
Curling at me in a crowded mall.

I try
I really do
I try not to hurt.
I do try not to think
I try to turn swiftly away
Away from painful thoughts
It doesn't work, but I keep trying
It's early days, and I am told it takes time,
I am trying, I am learning, I'm feeling every step.
I am also learning it's not okay to tell me how to feel.
The way to help me is to be there. I need time, not advice.

FIT IN

Fit in
Can't delete the D-word from conversations
That makes me a misfit
Must not cringe when the world is 'dying' to do something
Must not flinch when offered 'death' by chocolate
The world has no patience with grief
Try to smile
Do not embarrass
Don't answer questions that hurt,
Just change the topic
Take no offence
Because none is intended
Stay away from triggers
Or learn to block them
Look away.
Unsee.
Unhear.

Manorama Singh

SONI SINGH AND FAMILY

The Singh family lost their pillar, Manorama Singh, beloved wife, mother and grandmother. The family wrote about her:

Name: Manorama Singh…oops 'Maharaj'

Age: 70…oops ageless

Interests: Her children, flavour, nature, colour, devotion… oops *Joie de vivre* itself

My mother, my ma is the boldest and the most beautiful person I met. Her universe was her family. The bruises of life she took in her stride to raise us still jars us and has rankled our bonds with that part of the world that has hurt her. Her four daughters, she truly owned. And she would fight tooth and nail with the world for us. Her free laughter, her cheer, her determination, her discipline, her love for life is who she is. As she will always be there for us. She was truly proud of her children and loved her grandchildren. She was love itself for those who she "owned" and those who knew her. How do you live without love?

THE TRUTH | Kyraa Singh (09 years, Grand-daughter)

When one's loved one dies,
They forget how to laugh,
They forget how to smile,
Even their greatest strength turns into their fear,
After all, they've lost someone very dear!

YOU NEVER LEFT | Gayatri Singh (Daughter)

I am looking for you in the leaves of autumn
They are beautiful but not as solemn
I am looking for you in my dreams and memories
But I only feel you in the quiet of my habits
I am looking for you in the family video call
I am looking for your smile but I only feel my pain
I find your number and dial it again
I can't hear you and I only feel my pain
Always selfish in despair, did I forget you again
You gave me everything, did we give you all
I ask and I fail again.
Fail, no never, you never failed, you were a rock and you
instilled we never fail!
That's where you are, in that detail.
You raised us with all you got and that's everything we got
You were proud of us; we will be all you taught
Wish your smile lived longer
Your touch wish I could feel stronger
Your food was next to God
Your elegance was all so bold
You dressed up and showed up every day
Red and white and mustard and fawn and every colour you
would slay
The bindi and bangles and the heart of gold

Living On

You always stood out lo and behold
You made us laugh and healed our hearts
You made us strong and we shall play our parts.
We promise to continue but how I wish it would restart
You made us strong and we shall play our parts.
We will fall and rise, every minute every day
We will look and find in our hearts they say
We will ask and ask and maybe forgive one day
You lived to full and are happy, we pray.
You are a part of us and never went away.

A BAD DREAM | Sudha Singh (Daughter)

That voice still rankles
"Ma is gone Munni"
And I froze; its not true
And I decided its not true
I can hear her call out to me every other day
On my gate she stands and calls out my name
I bought a slice of sun in my porch for her
And I still can see her lying and basking in it in winter
I can see her on my sofa sipping the tea I made
In the not so small cup she likes
I can see her enjoying tea and maggi
With her grandchildren and me
That small ritual of togetherness every Friday
No, she is here with me everyday
I won't let her go, come what may
Ma, please please don't go I say.

ETERNAL LOVE | Sheo Shankar Singh (Husband)

She has vanished, and now become omnipresent, omniscient;
an essence, strewn all around us in the air,
in Nature and in all that she existed for;
become part and parcel of the Universe.
That's the truth.

It's natural you see
to behold her in all the air around you
and in all the natural substances,
trees and groves and leaves and flowers.
She will be looking at you from showering snows
and milky white solids around your home.
So my children nothing to worry;
celebrate with your mother
who is with you all around!

Her fearlessness, boldness, dressing were unmatched
with all her devotion to God,
she lived and died like a beauty queen.
To be true, I often felt jealous of her
when on some occasions
I looked at her and my own get-up, ashamed.

I never matched her,

however, I stood by her all the while.
I remember the last day of Ramnawmi
after she had finished her Puja
and went to the gate to find some girls to bestow gifts,
she looked gorgeous
never knowing, that it was her last visit to the gate
except when she finally left the house for hospital on fateful
28th of April.
Looked vacant at me, around the drawing room, paying her
devotion towards the puja room,
never knowing that she would not come back again.
No one had least idea that would be her final parting from
her home and children
whom she liked and loved so much.
Om Shantih!

GUILT | Soni Singh (Daughter)

It grows and cuts within
It hurts and scathes

For the love that remained
For the words, unspoken
For the pain suffered, undeservedly
For the habits, unchanged
For the dreams, unfulfilled
For the loneliness, unshared
For the life deserved, unlived

For the love that remained
For the words, unspoken

The guilt grows and cuts within
The guilt hurts and scathes.

DAUGHTER | Soni Singh (Daughter)

A daughter is born
Oh so dark
The beauty fades

The brothers go to college
But she has to marry

And she gives birth to daughters, only
One after the other
She is outcast
Unlucky

She nurtures them
Instils in them the fire and the dreams
That lie within

She loves and lives on
With pride
As the daughters realise the dreams.

Ananth Vignesh Sridar

GAYATHRI SRIDHAR

Gayathri lost her son Ananth about whom she shares:

Ananth Vignesh Sridar aka AVS was our first son. He went to Private, Montessori and Public schools. During Kindergarten he was given double promotion and was eligible to study 1st Grade. From a young age he showed his brilliance and excellence both academically and personally. He was knowledgeable about various subjects. He could solve all the problems in a unique way which made him a versatile and a dynamic person too. Here is what others said about Ananth:

Eve Chase (a school friend) — one that I first met in high school and have had the immense pleasure of keeping in contact with over the years. In the time that I knew Ananth, I watched him grow from a driven and passionate teenager to a clever, witty adult. Ananth will be dearly missed by myself, our entire TJ community, and the Secret Sofa Society.

Karin Lehnigk (a friend) — The world has lost such a brilliant guy, and I have lost such a great friend. He had amazing things ahead of him and I admired so much how he wielded his confidence like a weapon, making sure things got done and he got heard. I was looking forward to one day visiting him in Louisiana and touring the local geology (sand so much sand. Why on earth would he leave Texas to live in sand?)

with our different perspectives. I really enjoyed answering his questions about geology, and even more so when he'd send me a picture of Trigger (Ananth's Pet Dog) in return. I miss the conversations we'll never have, the things we'll never see again.

Steve Netemeyer (his Manager) — I had the pleasure of hiring Ananth into our Company, and he was part of my organization for the first three years of his career with the company. He had incredible technical skills, a wonderful way of connecting with others, and a unique sense of humor and wittiness. We missed him when he transferred to Port Allen, but we're excited for the future development opportunities, personal and professional that role would provide to him. Ananth touched many lives, as I'm sure he did in other contexts and phases of his life.

Liked and respected by all his school, collegemates to his office colleagues, Ananth was surrounded by a circle of people of all types. He had an enthusiastic individual attitude and this led to the quote stated by him, "No, I'm not done with Capstone yet."

"Can do spirit" was the attitude of all his work ethics from childhood to his angel anniversary.

GRIEF AND PEOPLE

Oh! World you have so many people.
Who are?
Mentors and Tutors
Professors and Teachers
Advisors and Counselors
Who teach
That grief is normal.

Well, they are all
General and Normal
Simple and Ordinary
Regular and Earthy.

Now, I must Battle my grief
With a Sword and Shield
Laugh out Loud,
Am not from a Royal Race.

Sword is my Action and
Shield is my Silence
To play (Battle) the Game of Grief

Yes, talk when needed
And act when wanted
Speak when asked
And attend to the needy

GRIEF AND ZODIAC SIGNS

Soul the Blueprint of Universe
Falls on this earth
To be born
With a Horoscope

They call it Soul Family
Rahu and Ketu — my ancestors
Sun and Moon — my parents
Mars and Mercury — my Siblings
Guru my Teacher and Professor
Venus my Merry and Joy
Finally, Saturn — My life actions

Here we all come
To live happily
with Sense to Battle our lives

Yes, I found it
We Know how to battle this grief —
Accept and Adore
Keep and Seek
Like and Love
Share and care
With soul sisters around…

GRIEF AND GRADUATION

Born in this world
To live a life
Enjoy my teenage
And experience marriage
To reproduce my children

Here I have graduated
In my school and college
As Mom and Parent

Oh! Is this a victory over my actions?
No and not at all
I am in school again to learn and graduate
In a place called bereavement

The Lesson is, to talk with all
Who have experienced
Struggling and battling with time
To make the best out of sense

See small to big picture
And comfort and pacify
Gives me the final graduation
To my Soul and Life

GRIEF: BATTLE AND RESOLUTION

Grief is pain and bitter
Still will remember and celebrate our loved ones

Grief is Sadness and remorse
We can Acknowledge and feel your presence

Grief eats our health from inside to out
Will live till our end to always think about you.

Grief thinks about food you liked
 As now you eat only to survive

Grief slowly steps into depression
  So that we stay fit enough to heal our soul

Greif is unpredictable
And it makes us a unique person

Lesson learned is to have patience
And spread love, kindness, compassion to all

Accept my reality
To emerge as Butterfly from the Cocoon

RAINBOW AND DEATH

Colors of the sky Painted by nature —
Glows in the young heart
And flows as energy in the old…
What do you really mean?
Colour of the sky
Or beautiful picture drawn
This is what comes to my mind,
Red is for restart now
Orange is to Omit all
Yellow is you live only once
Green is to go on
Blue is to bloom again
Indigo ways to gain an insight
Violet is to be vigilant
Colour of colours
emitted by the prism White color
and absorbed by the black within

Note: Meaning we are like that light emerged from darkness and ends
in the same way and in the middle the soul flies with rainbow colors.

FOR ALL THE GODS AND GURUS

For all the Gods and Gurus
wishing me well
Give a clue to live this life

Wonders of predictions
In the world of astrology
Tell me the truth of this plight

Religion and Spiritual
You give me the definition
For all sorts and kinds

Helpers and supporters
Of my Group
We discuss and cry

Therapist and Doctors
Give me medicine
From time to time

Now What is Life?
Live with breathing and eating
The pain of grief
And learn the process
To gain some relief

Rishikesh Sengupta

SHARMISTHA DASGUPTA

Sharmistha lost her father about whom she writes:

My father, Rishikesh,was a remarkable man, a small town boy who went on to achieve whatever he did on his own steam. Apart from being a successful professional, he started writing after we lost Ma, and went on to publish about 14 books and create over 200 odd paintings in about ten years. The most positive person I've known, he continues to be my role model along with my gentle Ma.

A DAUGHTER, A MOTHER TOO

Why does he call me Mother,
        I would wonder.
'Grandma's your mother Baba
        Then why me?'
'But you're my mother too', he would say
    Ruffling my curly black hair.

My young, handsome father,
Who bought me a chocolate every day
And held my bicycle as I learnt to ride,
Took me to the deep end of the pool
On his sturdy back,
And cheered me on as my little hands
Cut through the waters to reach the safety of his arms.

He didn't make me breakfast or tie my shoelaces,
But he held my hand as I walked to the school bus
And gently helped me up the steps.

Through the best and worst of the years
He stood by me,
Scouring College Street for hours on a hot summer
afternoon
For that one History book I thought I needed,
Struggling through broken tracks and the beating rain

To reach my hostel and take me home.
I had only to ask for the stars
And he would become God,
Touching the skies to bring me
My own Milky Way.

They didn't grow old together, my mother and he,
She left him suddenly one summer day,
Shocked and shattered, his spirit survived,
As he shook away the shackles of loss and pain
And stood up to face life as before.

And still held my hand as of old,
Made sure I kept his values alive,
In that everyday race
for the elusive pot of gold.

And then one day, felled by a deadly malady
He lay on the bed, a quiet shadow of himself,
And holding my hands, whispered,
"If I could only have, just another five years"

And as my tears mingled with his
And I promised to see him through —
My elderly, still so handsome Baba,
...I realised, with a sudden tightening within my chest,
That I had finally, after so many years,
Become the mother he had always sought in me.

REMEMBERING YOU

I remember you
  Every single day,
But without tears.
How can I cry for you
When I feel your presence
In everything I do?

Your assuring hand on my head
As I struggle to fill the pages,
That smile of childlike delight
That makes me a child too,
Your voice, amazingly tuneless
But not afraid to give us
Your own early morning rendition
Of the song of the moment,
The undying, everlasting self confidence
That kept you up and moving,
Despite and against the odds.

There you are,
In a very Mary Poppins like gesture,
Bringing it all out
With a flourish,
The endless stream of gifts,
The shimmering silks,

The rustling tussars,
The condiments and sweets
All the way from Calcutta,
All from a seemingly bottomless case,
That seldom carried anything
That was just yours…
I wish I had asked,
Even once,
At least, in jest,
If you had thought to bring
Clothes for yourself too.

I never cry for you,
When I look back
At those evenings
When I would run to meet you
On your return home,
Wonder if it was you
I would wait for,
Or the chocolate
You brought me every night.
My tears don't fall
When I remember those driving lessons,
All of sixteen,
I waited two years to get a license,
And you were the strictest teacher ever
Because it was me, and I had to be perfect.

I don't cry for you on your special days,
You wouldn't have wanted it that way
And nor would I,
Crying would mean I'd given you up,
Even when I know,
You are always by my side,
In everything I do.

WALK WITH ME, ONCE MORE

As a child I'd often wonder,
  How lonely I would be,
Without a doting father,
  To teach me A B C.

To guide my baby steps,
  To lift me if I fell,
To make me feel so brave
  Through stories he would tell.

The numbers seemed so easy
  Because he told me so,
That swim against the tide?
  Just an easy flow…

That hated walk each day
  To the school bus, uninviting,
An everyday adventure,
  Unknown, yet so exciting…

Because he walked with me
  And kissed my girly chin,
Without that loving hand,
  Where would I have been?

The road ahead now lonesome,
    I miss his smiling eyes,
Though unseen his presence,
    Somewhere beyond the skies.

If you could stand beside me,
    With your stories yet untold,
And make me brave once more
    As newer paths unfold…?

Reba Sengupta

Sharmistha also lost her mother. About her, she writes:

My mother, Reba, was the most selfless, compassionate, honest human being I've ever met. Not divine but definitely a person close to Godliness. Her untimely passing left us devastated and affected our lives like nothing else did.

MISSING YOU

The fragrance of your tresses
  As you kissed my girly chin,
Soft fingers,turmeric stained,
  As you gently tucked me in,

The tinkling spoons and bangles
  As you brewed the morning tea,
That whiff of soap and sweat
  As your arms reached out to me.
You smelt of rain soaked earth,
  You smelt of baking bread,
Your eyes forever telling
  And yet so much unsaid.

These images so real
  The years we've left behind,
A touch of yesterday
  Now captured in my mind.

Your smile, in black and silver,
  On my bedroom wall,
But Ma, I'll wait forever
  To hear once more that call.

Across the distant skies

I'll reach beyond the trees,
And find your missing fragrance
    In the whispering of the breeze.

You'll comb my wrinkles out
    You'll kiss my dimpled chin,
Your little girl once more,
    As you gently tuck me in.

MOTHER'S DAY

You never had to remind me of your love,
Not on a special day,
I just knew it,
When your smile lit up
Those eyes looking into my own.
I cried when you reprimanded me
For silly things
I did ,or did not do,
But when I held your face
In my little baby arms
And saw you break into a smile
Because I'd asked you to,
I could feel the warmth of your heart
Seeping into my own.

We never had a Mother's Day or a daughter's day,
growing up,
But you waited hours to lunch with me after school,
Sat up late into the night as I finished my homework,
Snuggled into my bed at early dawn,
To make sure I wouldn't go back to sleep
Without doing my revisions,
Spent sleepless nights
Making sure mine were not,
Before my semesters.

Scolded me and loved me,
Spoilt me and disciplined me
With equal fervour,
And made every day
An adventure of sorts,
A special one,
One, perhaps, we could give a new name to,
One, perhaps, I would call
A mother's day.
And you could call,
…A daughter's.

OF THE SONGS WE HUMMED TOGETHER

Often, in my dreams,
I am little again,
My small fingers
Reaching out to touch
That deep scar on your chin.
What is this, I ask.
A reminder
Of my wilder years,
You say with a smile.
But a mother is never naughty,
I whisper, after a shocked silence,
Oh,I improved after I became one,
You giggle,
And I giggle with you,
Our laughters mingling
As a mother's and daughter's
Always will.

I can hear you,
Singing, as you make breakfast,
Words often replaced
With an ambiguous lalala
Because you don't remember,
The heat of the stove
Bringing a flush

To your beloved face,
The heightened colour
Adding to the warmth
That we so love,
I can feel it,
Too real to be a dream.

I have felt it over the years,
Ever since…
A fleeting brush against my head,
A whisper no one else can hear,
A finger stroking
My troubled brow,
Promising an eternity
Someday,
Of humming lost numbers,
Of being naughty together,
Of our laughters mingling,
As only a mother's
…and daughter's will.

Divakar Sinha

SWATI PAL

Swati is no stranger to loss. She had suffered the loss of her father soon after she turned eighteen. And she had seen how her world, all that she took for granted, the way she envisioned her future, suddenly changed overnight. She has written often about her father whom she called Baba and on one occasion she wrote —

Many people, in fact all who know Baba, say that I am a lot like him. Swarthy of complexion, brown eyes, broad smile, loud laugh, carrying voice and a quick though short temper. I love that I look like him, especially given that like all youngest born, I used to be teased that I have been picked up from the...well, whatever!

My Baba was a brilliant and committed Army doctor — I put the two together because his love for his profession as a doc was matched by his passion for the olive green. He was an expert swimmer, cyclist, could ride a horse and was a great skier. Sadly, I did not inherit that gene. He sketched including charcoal paintings which are simply unbelievable — I believe my few forays into this zone have been fairly good so I guess I got that ability from Baba. He was very social and liked nothing more than a lot of people home and loads of good food (and my mom is just a far out cook). That sociable nature too I think I have inherited. Ma was his beloved queen and we daughters his princesses. Well, he was and is the uncrowned king of all our lives.

Baba took many field postings after I was born to ensure that at least I was not uprooted every three years. So a lot that I know of my Baba is through stories narrated by my sisters and other family members. I have hoarded those stories and clung to them so that in a sense, he is sharper in my mind than perhaps to many others.

It's been long years since he left in body, I was only 18. But he will never leave my heart and my mind. He has taught me a lot by being who he was. A large hearted, compassionate man, devoted to his family, a workaholic, bearing pain stoically, versatile....Brig Mahadeb Pal, VSM, my father. I am so proud to be your daughter. And I hope you have your comb in hand...I remember how you would always comb your hair (in the two tufts on either side of your head) in excitement, when any of us achieved something...I hope I give you some reason to do so.

Stay well and please be with Mohan.

And who is Mohan? Mohan is Divakar Sinha, Swati's son whom she lost in body on 11th June, 2019. It is difficult for her to write about Mohan though through her poems she shares what he has been like. This is what Mudit Goel (a friend of Mohan) wrote about him —

GOEL.MUDIT304 Posts

Divakar was the happiest when he was with his friends. I miss his random 2 AM calls to talk about football. I miss his laugh, the most expressive and genuine laugh I ever heard. I miss his ability to irritate me and cherish every moment of it. I miss our taunting messages after football matches. I miss him insisting that we come to gather at his house every time he returned from college. It has been almost 3 years, and I still miss everything about him.

His passing bought us all closer together. The pain would

have been too much to bear alone, and I was fortunate to have the best friends one could ever ask for. The irony is all he ever wanted was for all of us to stick together, and in a way he made sure we will. Divakar had the purest of hearts, and he was the best friend one could ever have. I was lucky to have him in my life. I wish I had appreciated him more. Now when Liverpool win it doesn't feel as bad because at least it's making him happy somewhere.

I learnt a lot from him. I learnt how to be the biggest cheerleader for my friends. I learnt how to celebrate others' successes like my own. I learnt fierce loyalty. Basically, I learned how to be a better friend. His death gave me a lot of perspective about what really matters in life. He will always remain a source of strength for me. Giving his eulogy was the toughest thing I have ever done in my life.

He really was the best of us, and someday I hope to live up to the high standard he set. If he could see me now I know he would have been really happy and proud.

I never believed in an afterlife. I always thought that we die, and that's it. Now, I hope there is something, somewhere we get to grow old with Divakar, as it should have been.

JUST TO BE ABLE

Just to be able
To talk
While we walk
About some guy
In class
Who was cheeky
With the Prof,
And you laugh
When I chastise.

Just to be able
To talk
At the dining table
Where I
Try to shovel in
Spoonful's of rice
Into your mouth
To speed up lunch
And you clutch
My wrist
As you want
To tell
Your tale.

Just to be able
To talk

About this song
That film
How Liverpool FC
Is faring
And a book
By Chetan Bhagat
That even you
Cannot digest
And of course
The plan
For what to order
For dinner.

Just to be able
To talk
Just to be able
To hear
You laugh
And chatter
And call out
'Grub'
Or
'Shukadoo'
Or
'Hoora Hara'
Apart from
Ma and Mommy,
That you
Call me.

Oh just
To be able
Oh just
To be
Oh just.

MY STORY TO TELL

You are my story
To tell
And tell it
I will.
Over
And over
And more
Again and again.

You may call
Me a bore,
Dislike
My use of gore,
But tell it
I will.

With tears
And watery smiles
With screams
And sighs
And pain
And pride
I will tell.

Regardless
Of who listens
Who casts me aside.

For you
Are my story
To tell
And that
Even you
Cannot take away
From me
Or deny.

FOOLING THE WORLD

Each moment
Of time
Gone by
Is crowded
With sights
And sounds
And tastes
And colours
And feelings
Of body
And heart,
Of things
We said
And did
Together.
You and I
And ours.

They whirl
And swirl
And ebb
And flow,
Till tears
And screams
Of agony

And the clutch
Of my head
In the palms
Of my hands
Attempt in vain
To stem
The bleeding
Heart,
And
In a stupor
I watch
The shadows
On the ceiling
Of the darkened room

And day breaks.

And I pick
Her up
Battered
Bruised
Dead,
And I
Make her walk
And talk
And smile
And laugh
And think.
And fool the world.

THE IRONY

The irony.
Of weightless tears
And the weight
Of the pain
They carry.
Of eyes wide open
And the vision
Clouded
By blinding tears.

Living the irony
Every minute.

I am
The irony.

FOREVER NIGHT

The other night
Night said to me,
'I dread
The break
Of day.
It robs me
Off my identity.
My arms encircle
The world
And wrapped
In my warm embrace,
All creatures sleep
At peace
Their cares
Put away.

But
With every passing hour
I feel
Myself diminish
Till
I am erased,
And then
The wait
For my time'.

Living On

Her voice trembled
As she spoke.

I stared
At her.
For me
There is only
Night.

And yes
I dread
The break of day,

It means
I am forced
To see it through
Even as I carry
The night
In my heart
On my shoulders
And in my eyes.
I too wait
For my time
Which I know
Is not
Of this earth
But
Of another abode.

What could be worse
Than the waiting
That I face
As tick tock
Goes
The clock

Interminably.

I am held captive,
Caged
In my body

My heart weeps
Uncontrollably

WHAT FOOLS WE BE

What fools
We be!
Calling out
To those dead
To be
With us
Talk
To us
Embrace us.

The living
Often forget
To be
With us
Talk
To us
Embrace us,
Unless jolted
By pangs
Of conscience
Or persuasion.

And yet
We crave
Those not

On earth
And unable
And those
On earth
And unwilling.

What fools
We be.

Swati Pal with her father, Brig Mahadeb Pal

SWATI PAL, Professor and Principal, Janki Devi Memorial College, University of Delhi, writes poetry when she is not teaching or completing her administrative tasks. Apart from poems in anthologies, she has a collection entitled, *In Absentia* (Hawakal Publishers, 2021). Her academic pursuits include performance and culture studies, education, academic and creative writing. She translates from Hindi to English. Of all her roles, she loves that of *mom*.

About the Contributors

Dr. Bhramar Choudhury, retired Prof of English, writes in English, Bangla, Hindi and Urdu. She has a junior diploma in Persian and many translated works of Hindi and Bangla poetry. She has received recognition from Bihar Bangla Academy for *Baluka Bhara Akti Nadi* (translation of Prof Jabir Husain's *Ek Nadi Ret Bhari*) and by Bihar Rashtrabhasha Parishad for her contribution to Hindi literature.

Anita Panda is a Mumbai-based passionate writer, poet, blogger, lyricist, feminist, spiritualist, founder of 'Single & Strong' support group, active member of 'Lean-In-Mumbai' network, a spunky warrior, crusader and incorrigible dreamer. She believes in building a gender equal and progressive world. She has compiled a collection of poems by her brother, Surya, called *Genesis*.

Jaya Ayyappa has been a psychotherapist for over 20 years. She is also a corporate trainer and a passionate sexuality educator. She believes in removing the taboo around the topics of sexuality. She has been a speaker at many conferences.

Jaya Prasad, Assistant Professor of English, B.S. College, Patna, has composed poems lamenting the untimely demise of her elder sister, Divya Prasad. The poems are an expression of love as well as anguish that she sees as eternal and are an outcome of deeply felt emotions, best articulated through poetry.

Seema Tejaswee Rao is a Gurgaon-based fitness and outdoors enthusiast who enjoys hiking and bird photography. She tries to live simply, practicing minimalism, respecting all life forms, following a zero waste and vegan lifestyle. Seema created "In

Our Hearts Forever," a support group for bereaved mothers which is her biggest strength and support.

The contributors for Manorama are her grandchild, **Kyraa**; her children, **Sudha** (HR Professional; PMIR, XLRI Jamshedpur), **Soni** (Co-Founder & Partner, VGA Legal; Chevening Scholar), and **Gayatri** (Sr. Reisurance Professional; M.Sc., Hindu College); and her husband, **Sheo Shankar**.

Gayathri Sridhar holds a Master's Degree in Public Administration and is a professional paralegal. She loves reading all kinds of books and is geared towards Metaphysics as a concept. She believes that learning is a lifelong process and this has made her find new ways and means to live life.

Sharmistha Dasgupta, born and brought up in West Bengal and currently a resident of Hyderabad, socially active and an animal lover has been touched by loss at an early age but has never ceased to believe in the inherent goodness of life.

www.ingramcontent.com/pod-product-compliance
Lightning Source LLC
Chambersburg PA
CBHW051455130726
47987CB00005B/2323